D060452?

LET'S PLAY
Baseball

Karen Durrie

www.av2books.com

AV² provides enriched content that supplements and complements this book. Weigl's AV² books strive to create inspired learning and engage young minds in a total learning experience.

Your AV² Media Enhanced books come alive with...

 Audio
Listen to sections of the book read aloud.

 Video
Watch informative video clips.

 Embedded Weblinks
Gain additional information for research.

 Try This!
Complete activities and hands-on experiments.

 Key Words
Study vocabulary, and complete a matching word activity.

 Quizzes
Test your knowledge.

 Slide Show
View images and captions, and prepare a presentation.

...and much, much more!

Go to **www.av2books.com**, and enter this book's unique code.

BOOK CODE

S 1 9 2 2 3 5

AV² by Weigl brings you media enhanced books that support active learning.

Published by AV² by Weigl
350 5th Avenue, 59th Floor New York, NY 10118
Website: www.av2books.com   www.weigl.com

Durrie, Karen.
 Baseball / Karen Durrie.
   p. cm. -- (Let's play)
 ISBN 978-1-61690-937-6 (hardcover : alk. paper) -- ISBN 978-1-61690-583-5 (online)
 1. Baseball--Juvenile literature. I. Title.
 GV867.5.D87 2011
 796.357--dc23
 [B]
                              2011023427
Printed in the United States of America in North Mankato, Minnesota
1 2 3 4 5 6 7 8 9 0 15 14 13 12 11

062011
WEP030611

Project Coordinator: Karen Durrie Art Director: Terry Paulhus

Weigl acknowledges Getty Images as the primary image supplier for this title.

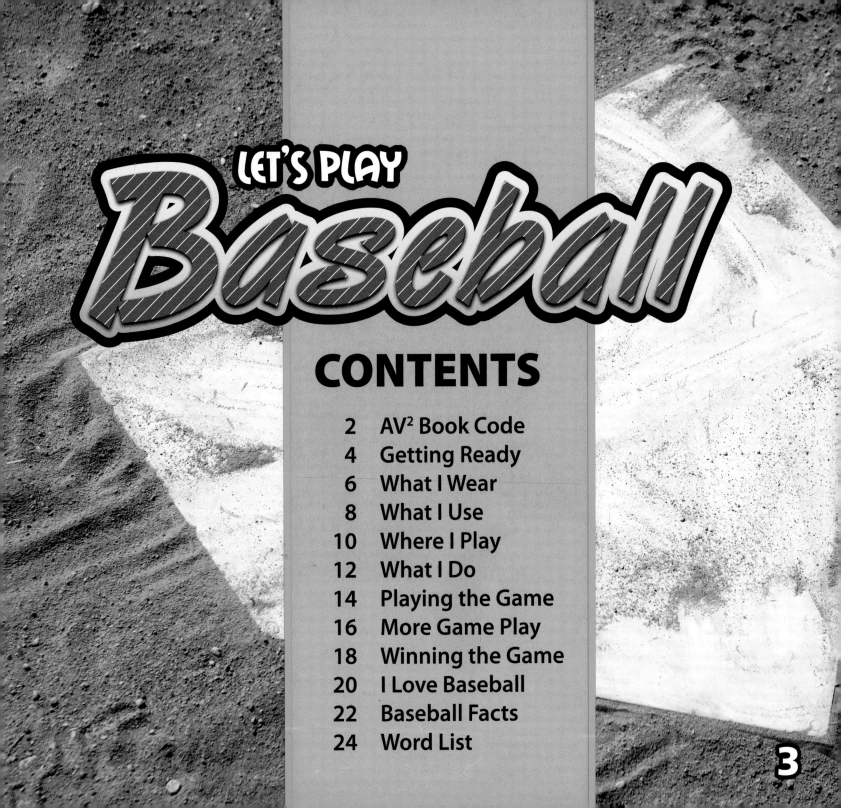

LET'S PLAY
Baseball

CONTENTS

I love baseball.
I am going to play
baseball today.

4

Like a PRO

Some kids play a kind of baseball called T-ball.

5

I get dressed
for baseball.
I put on my blue jersey.

6

A team wears the same color jersey.

I have a baseball glove.
I wear it
to catch the ball.

8

Like a PRO

I wear my glove
in the outfield.

I meet my team. We play catch before the game.

Playing catch
and stretching
warm me up.

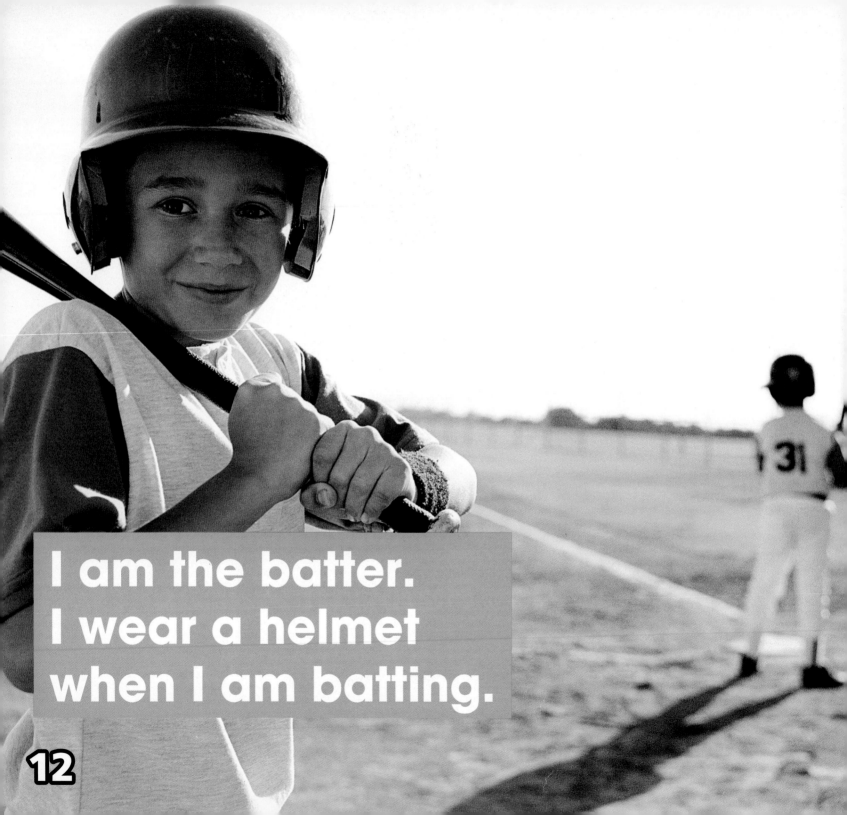

I am the batter.
I wear a helmet
when I am batting.

12

A helmet keeps
my head safe.

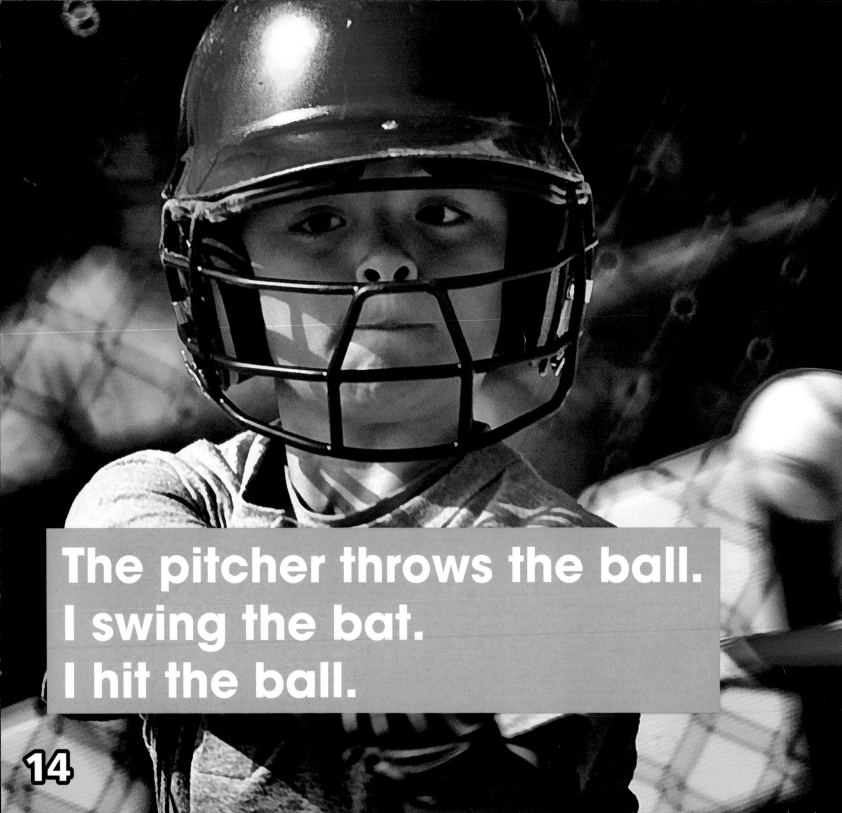

The pitcher throws the ball.
I swing the bat.
I hit the ball.

14

Like a PRO

If I do not
hit the ball,
it is called
a strike.

15

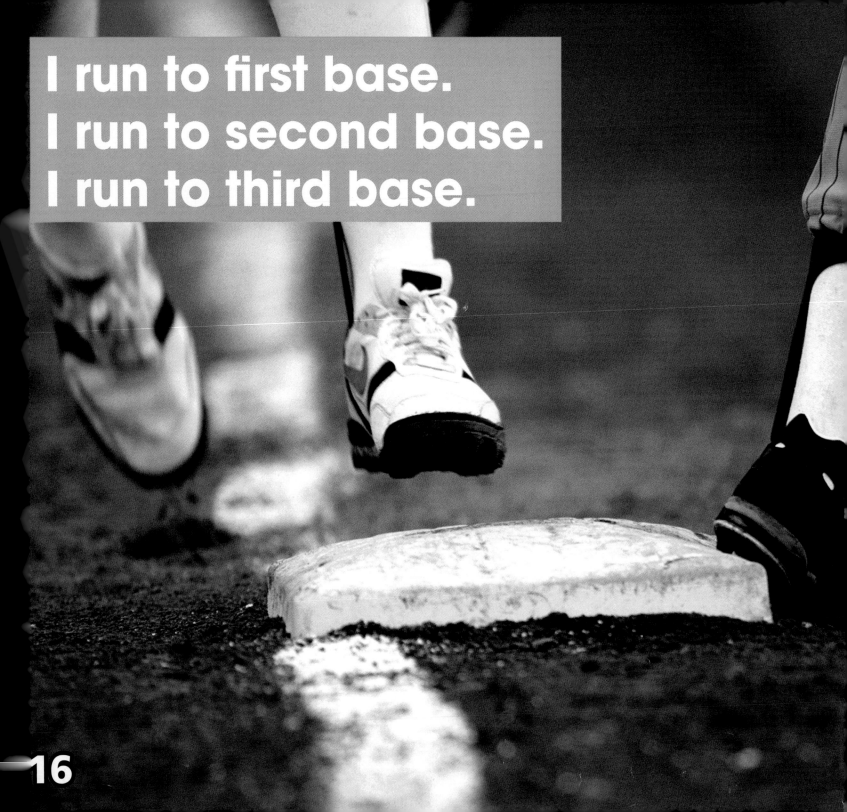

I run to first base.
I run to second base.
I run to third base.

A baseball
field is called
a diamond.

I slide into home base.
I have scored a run.
My team cheers.

18

Teams take turns on the field.

I love baseball.

BASEBALL FACTS

This page provides more detail about the interesting facts found in the book.
Simply look at the corresponding page number to match the fact.

Pages 4-5

T-ball, or Tee Ball, is often a child's first introduction to baseball. Players hit the ball off a batting tee.

Pages 6–7

Numbers on uniforms help people to identify players at a distance. Originally in baseball, the numbers related to the batting order of players. Now, players may choose a number because it is their favorite, or they think it is lucky.

Pages 8–9

Baseball gloves are made of leather or synthetic materials. The fingers are sewn together so that the glove forms a pocket that makes it easier to catch and keep the ball inside.

Pages 10–11

Cold muscles are stiff, and sudden twisting and turning of them can cause injury. Warming and stretching muscles before baseball can reduce the risk of injury. Warm muscles are more flexible and produce energy faster. Baseball involves fast bursts of running and requires strength for batting, catching, and throwing.

Pages 12–13

Players at bat wear lightweight plastic batting helmets to protect the head and ears. They keep the helmets on when running bases. When a team is in the outfield, players wear baseball caps to shield their eyes from the Sun.

Pages 14–15

There are many rules of play in baseball. If a batter strikes out three times, their turn at bat is over. If a fielder catches a batted ball before it hits the ground, the batter is out. If a fielder tags a runner with the ball before they get to the next base, that player is out. Umpires watch closely and make sure players follow the rules.

Pages 16–17

The baseball diamond is separated into two parts—the infield and the outfield. On the infield, batters run from base to base, and the pitcher throws the ball from the pitcher's mound. Dirt or shale make up the infield around the pitcher's mound. The outfield is a grassy area behind the infield.

Pages 18–19

There are many positions on the baseball field. Pitchers throw the ball to batters from the mound. Catchers squat behind the batters and catch the ball if it is not hit. Base players stand on the infield to try to catch the ball and tag runners out. Outfielders catch balls hit into the outfield.

Pages 20–21

If a batter makes a fair hit and runs all the bases without stopping, it is a home run. If there are runners on all the bases when the batter scores a home run, and all of the players run home, it is called a grand slam.

WORD LIST

Research has shown that as much as 65 percent of all written material published in English is made up of 300 words. These 300 words cannot be taught using pictures or learned by sounding them out. They must be recognized by sight. This book contains 37 common sight words to help young readers improve their reading fluency and comprehension. This book also teaches young readers several important content words. These words are paired with pictures to aid in learning and improve understanding.

Page	Sight Words First Appearance	Page	Content Words First Appearance
4	I, play, to	4	baseball, today
5	a, also, kind, of, some	5	kids, T-ball
6	for, get, on, put, my	6	jersey
7	same, the	7	color, team
8	have, it, to	8	ball, glove
9	in	9	outfield
10	before, we	10	game
11	and, me, up	11	catch
12	when	12	batter, helmet
13	head, keeps	13	head
15	do, if, is, not	14	bat, pitcher
16	first, run, second	15	strike
18	home, into	16	base
19	take	17	diamond, field
		18	home, run
		19	turns

Check out av2books.com for activities, videos, audio clips, and more!

1 Go to av2books.com

2 Enter book code

S 1 9 2 2 3 5

3 Fuel your imagination online!

www.av2books.com